Let's Talk About
GOSSIPING

Grolier Enterprises Inc. offers a varied selection of both
adult and children's book racks. For details on ordering,
please write: Grolier Enterprises Inc., Sherman Turnpike,
Danbury, CT 06816, Attn: Premium Department.

Let's Talk About
GOSSIPING

By JOY BERRY

Illustrated by John Costanza
Edited by Kate Dickey
Designed by Abigail Johnston

GROLIER ENTERPRISES CORP.

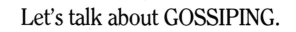

Let's talk about GOSSIPING.

When you say unkind things about people
to other people, you are gossiping.

When you say untrue things about people to other people, you are gossiping.

Gossiping can hurt the people
you gossip about.

The things you say may cause them to feel bad
about themselves.

The people you gossip about can be hurt
in another way.

The things you say may cause others
to treat them unkindly.

Gossiping can hurt you.

Others may think that you are unkind
if you say unkind things.

They may not like you.

They may not want to be around you.

Gossiping can hurt you in another way.

Others may think you are dishonest
if you say things that are not true.

They may not trust you.

They may not believe anything you say.

Gossiping can hurt others and it can hurt you.
You should not gossip. Here is a good rule for you
to follow

**If you can't say something nice,
don't say anything at all.**

Some people may ask you questions
about other people so that you will gossip.
Do not gossip when this happens.
Do these things instead.

Kindly tell the other people
that you would rather not answer
their questions. Then suggest that you talk
about something else.

Do not try to get other people to say things that are unkind or untrue.

Do not ask questions that will cause them to gossip.

Do not listen to people who want to gossip to you. Do these things instead.

Kindly tell them that you do not want to hear gossip.

Go away from them if they continue gossiping.

When people gossip about you,
it may hurt you or make you angry.
You may want to gossip about them.

When people gossip about you,
don't gossip about them.
Do these things instead.

Go to the people. Kindly talk to them.
Then, ask them to not gossip about you again.

Try to solve your problems.

You may need to ask someone
to help you do this.

When you do not know or understand people,
you may want to gossip about them.
Do not gossip about them.
Do these things instead.

Introduce yourself to the people.
Get to know them and be kind to them.

It is important that you treat other people the way you want to be treated.

If you do not want people to gossip about you, you should not gossip about them.